Woodworking with Children

Translated by Susan Beard

Photography: Anette Grunditz and Ulf Erixon
Illustrations and diagrams: Ulf Erixon

First published in Swedish as *Snickra med och till barn*
by Forma Books in 2012
First published in English by Floris Books in 2014

British Library CIP data available
ISBN 978-178250-039-1
Printed in Singapore

Woodworking with Children

Anette Grunditz and Ulf Erixon

Floris Books

Contents

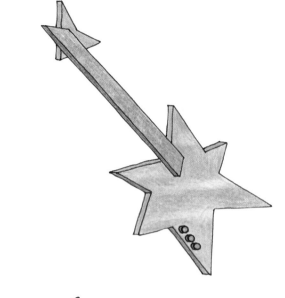

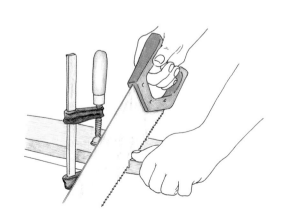

Play Equipment 48

House and Garden 60

Further reading 76

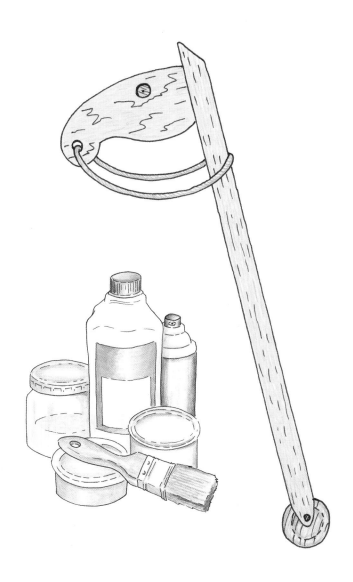

Disclaimer – please read carefully

Kindergarten children (up to the age of six or seven) should experience the physical qualities of wood directly, with their own hands, and slightly older children will be able to handle basic tools safely, understand their principles, and feel the connection between their energy and the tool's function. Many of the tasks in this book are suitable for making with children, but please remember that working with tools and wood can be dangerous. The Publisher can accept no liability for damages and injury of any kind. Before using any tool with which you are unfamiliar, consult its operating instructions and, if necessary, seek instruction by a qualified person for appropriate safety techniques.

Foreword

This book aims to inspire anyone who wants to get creative with children and woodwork. There are projects here for absolute beginners and for those who want more of a challenge, but you don't need to be an experienced carpenter to tackle any of them, nor do you need expensive tools or materials. We start with tips that will make things easy for those who are less experienced, but if you've already done a bit of woodworking and have a basic knowledge of materials, equipment and tools, you can skip over the early chapters and pick a woodworking project.

Once you've started to get the hang of things you'll find it easy to improvise and design your own versions of our projects. There is no right or wrong when it comes to design. Artistic freedom is important – bear this in mind when one detail or another doesn't turn out quite as planned. A positive approach allows creativity to flow. An object is much more fun if it looks homemade rather than shop-bought. Children and adults alike will be impressed when they see the car you've crafted actually works: when its wheels turn even though it isn't a scale model of a Ferrari. In a child's world, nothing stops a wooden block with wheels turning into a turbo-charged Grand Prix winner. With five children in our family, we have seen repeatedly that homemade toys stimulate their imagination, and are ultimately more educational than lifelike copies of adult objects.

Woodworking with Children contains thirty fun projects, which can be adapted according to your own needs and ideas. There are simple games and indoor toys, along with outdoor play equipment like a swing set and a sandpit. There are also practical items, such as a coat stand and a bird feeder, for use around the house or garden.

Children will be able to make some of these projects themselves with a bit of supervision. With others, they can play an assistant role, learning through observation as you make something they can then use.

We hope you and the children around you will have lots of fun with these projects, and will enjoy the pride that comes from being able to say: 'I made this myself!'

Anette Grunditz and Ulf Erixon

Tool icons

Next to each project in this book you will see circular icons. These icons indicate the tools you will need, and give you an idea of approximately how many steps are involved in the project: the more icons, the more steps.

Saw — Sawing required. There are many different kinds of saws, including handsaws and electric circular saws.

Ruler — Measuring required. You will need a folding rule, tape measure or ruler.

Drill — Drilling or inserting screws required. You will need a power drill or perhaps a screwdriver.

Wood adhesive — Glueing required.

Hammer — Hammering nails required.

Mitre square — A mitre square is required, to make an exact right angle.

Brush — Painting or oiling required.

File — Sanding required. You will need a sanding tool or sandpaper.

Getting Started

Materials

Anyone going to a timber yard for the first time is quite likely to be confused by the huge storage units filled with varying types of planks and boards. Staff are often helpful and obliging, so don't be afraid to ask for what you want. If they don't stock what you need, get advice about what you could use instead. There's no such thing as a stupid question!

The materials we use for the projects in this book can be found in most well-stocked timber yards, DIY (home improvement) centres or hobby stores, and perhaps even in garden centres. We also sometimes use kits or ready-made or partially-made items, such as wheels, batons and edgings.

Planed timber, stripwood and blocks

Planed timber (or planed lumber) is wood that has been planed down to give a smooth finish. Stripwood (or wood planks) is square-edged timber in long pieces; a versatile and practical material. Sheet plywood is a manufactured material. It consists of panels made of thin layers of wood veneer. You will also see batten mentioned in the book – this is a thin strip of wood, often used for covering or strengthening joins.

Standard dimensions for planed planks of timber vary from country to country. If you cannot find pre-cut timber that matches the dimensions suggested in this book, some timber yards or home improvement stores will cut to your specifications. You could also adapt the project to the size of materials you can get, choosing pre-

cut planed timber with measurements that are close to the suggested ones.

Blocks of wood are easy to get hold of. Save offcuts from other carpentry projects or use a rule and saw a few different-sized blocks off a planed piece of timber. Children have an incredible ability to create something imaginary from simple shapes. You'll soon see how a few blocks can be turned into cars, trains, towns and many other things.

From an early age, children are drawn to building towers with infinite care; they will invest a lot of time and effort on such constructions. Generally they are also delighted to send the entire creation toppling down. Fortunately, blocks are very durable toys.

It's not a big step from a block to a functional object, and children will enjoy the transformation. Using a drill you can quickly and easily make a simple candleholder or a pencil stand.

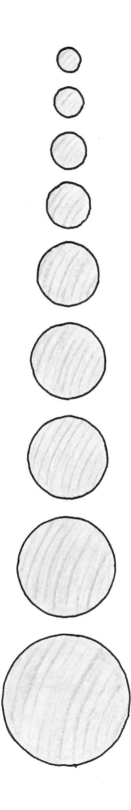

Dowel rods

As with the varying dimensions of stripwood and planed timber, dowel rods come in many different diameters. In this book we use a great variety of sizes. Dowel has a wide range of uses, so it's a good idea to buy several different sizes to keep in your workshop.

It's easy to do magic with dowel! Saw a 40 cm (16 in) length of 12 mm (½ in) diameter dowel. Paint it black and white with hobby paint and – abracadabra! – you have made a magic wand! If you want the painted lines to be perfectly straight, use the white paint first, wait until it is completely dry, then put masking tape around each white end before painting the rest black.

There are often round shapes in the projects in this book. For example, we use dowel of various diameters to make wheels. All you need to do is cut the desired wheel thickness and drill a hole in the centre. You can also buy ready-made wheels in hobby shops. They are a little more expensive than making your own, but they often have a better finish and look more like tyres.

To make a **skipping rope**, saw two pieces of dowel for handles and drill a hole through the centre of each one to hold a length of rope or cord. The rope should be long enough to be taut if the skipper stands on the middle and holds both the ends up to his or her armpits. Secure the rope by tying a knot at each end, making sure it is large enough not to slip through the hole. You can gauge the length of the handles by measuring across the palm that is going to hold them and adding a few centimetres either side to allow for a firm grip. Choose dowel with a diameter that feels comfortable to hold. For an adult hand, 25 mm

(1 in) is suitable, with a handle length of about 15 cm (6 in). For a keen young skipper with a smaller hand, a smaller diameter of dowel feels better to hold. Remember that you have to drill through the dowel, so choose a circumference big enough to allow for this.

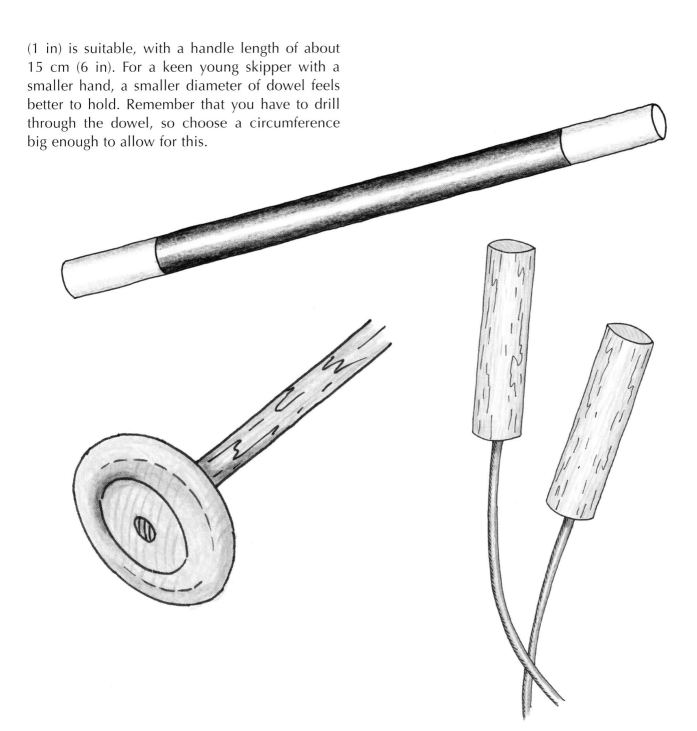

Tools

Tools can be really expensive but often cheaper versions are perfectly good for hobby carpenters. Higher priced tools are designed for professionals, who handle them for eight hours a day. You won't need that level of strength and ergonomic design.

Balance this with an eye for tools that will last. Sometimes when you buy the very cheapest tools available all you get is frustration: drill bits bend, pliers pinch your hand and badly-made hammers can't even extract a nail.

Below, you'll find a list of tools and equipment that would be handy to have if you are embarking on the projects in this book. To keep them tidy we show you how to make a toolbox – a good starter project from which you can move on to bigger things.

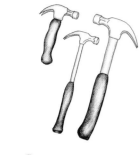

Hammer

There are many different types of hammer, each with its own purpose, but for the woodwork projects in this book, you can manage very well with an all-round hammer such as the ones illustrated here. They are called claw hammers. Their useful curved end pulls out incorrectly hammered nails.

Saw

If you do a lot of woodwork it is much easier to own or borrow or share an electric circular saw, but you can still achieve a lot using a traditional handsaw. Other types of saw include a bow saw for cutting thick timber, a hacksaw for metal, and a Japanese trim saw for precision work and fine cutting.

Measuring tape

All credit to measuring by eye, but at times it's vital to get lengths exact. Carefully measured wood will produce neater, longer-lasting objects. It's worth buying a measuring tape or a folding rule if you don't have access to one. Find one with a millimetre (fractions of an inch) scale.

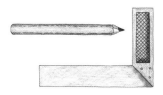

Mitre square and carpenter's pencil

A mitre square lets you check the accuracy of angles, but is also handy for using like a ruler to measure short lengths. A good carpenter's pencil will have a wide lead that never breaks and is strong enough to mark unplaned surfaces.

Adhesive

When you need to strengthen an object that definitely must not come apart at the joins, nails and screws can be complemented with that reliable standby: adhesive. This will give the pieces two forms of attachment and a firmer hold. Adhesive is also ideal for joins that are too small for nails or screws. There are various kinds of woodworking adhesive, some specially labelled for indoor use, outdoor use and even for winter use. They generally dry within a few hours.

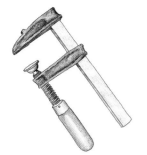

Screw clamp

Alongside adhesive, a screw clamp is a real winner when it comes to creating durable objects. It is used to hold parts together while adhesive sets. There are different types of clamps: the most popular one is the quick action clamp, but there are also G-clamps, hand-screw clamps and many others.

Knife

A sharp knife can be useful for adult carpenters in all sorts of ways. Apart from the fact that it is perfect for sharpening your carpenter pencil, you can also use it to carve details or bevel edges. Make sure the knife has a bolster that guards your fingers from slipping towards the blade. Blunt knives are unsafe because risks escalate when you apply too much pressure. Take care of your knife, sharpen it as required and store it in a place out of the reach of curious small fingers. Keep a close eye on it when you are doing woodwork with children. There is a good range of knife sheaths to choose from, with belt loops and fastenings so that you can carry it at all times.

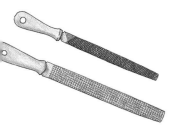

Rasp and file

These filing tools are used for fine or coarse wood shaping. A rasp leaves a coarse finish and is used to remove wood rapidly and make fast progress. For a smoother finish and greater precision there are smaller files in various thicknesses and shapes: rectangular, triangular, half-round and round. The type of file to choose depends on personal taste and how the item is going to be used. Smooth, even surfaces prevent both big and little hands from getting splinters.

Pliers

Pliers such as pincers, combination pliers and side cutters are suitable for extracting or cutting off nails, and for other purposes.

Power drill

Professionals usually view the nail gun and the power drill as gifts from above. It is undeniably a pleasure and a timesaver to drill holes and insert screws using a power tool. Power drills with rechargeable batteries vary greatly in price. As a rule, the battery of a cheaper machine doesn't last as long as a more expensive model, but if it's not going to be used much then an inexpensive model is probably perfectly acceptable.

Drill bit holder

This is an attachment to a power drill that magnetically holds a screw in place, from when you place the screw on the drill bit until the screw is driven home. It's worth a fortune not to have to run up and down the ladder, fetching dropped screws. The drill bit holder makes it easy to change drill bits to fit the various types of slots on screw heads.

Drill bits

You could almost say there is a drill bit for every occasion. There are different lengths and thicknesses, as well as shapes, to fit the various screw head driver slots, all intended to suit every kind of material: bits for wood drills, steel drills and large hole drills, to name just a few.

Techniques

Holding the hammer

A hammer that is the correct size and a comfortable weight is a great start. A heavy hammer is good, but it shouldn't be so heavy that it strains your wrist. Try to hold it as close to the bottom of the handle as possible: more swing means more force. Watch out for hammer handles that feel too big for your hand – they can easily cause cramp.

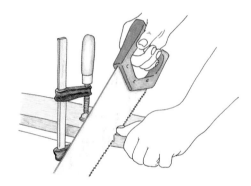

Sawing

If you use a clamp to hold the piece you are sawing in place, you can saw far more confidently. Use your thumb to support the saw for the first few strokes while you make a small cut. The small cut will then keep the saw in place; once you have made it, carry on sawing using long strokes.

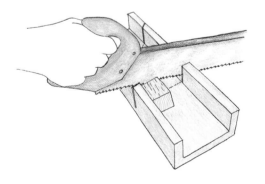

Using a mitre box

Use a mitre box when you want to cut precise angles, such as 90° or 45°. Place the piece to be cut in the box, lining it up with the appropriate slot. Place the saw blade in the slot and begin to saw.

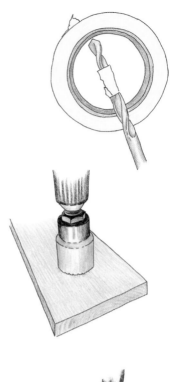

MASKING TAPE

Masking tape is very handy, having many uses aside from masking off areas when painting. For example, if you are drilling and need to be careful not to drill too deep, you can measure the depth on the drill bit then mark it using a piece of tape, which will indicate when to stop. Masking tape is easy to remove as its adhesive property is not permanent, and it doesn't tend to leave a sticky residue.

HOLE SAW

As the name suggests, a hole saw is used for making large holes. It can feel difficult at times to get through the material. Try moving the drill slightly from side to side as you drill.

INSERTING SCREWS

When you put a screw into wood there is always a risk that the wood will split. It can help – and at times it is necessary – to first drill a hole with a drill bit that is a little smaller than the screw you are going to use.

AVOIDING WOOD SPLITS

One tip that might help avoid wood splitting is to drill from the back of the wood until the point of the drill bit goes all the way through. Then turn the piece of wood over, place the drill in the small exit hole and drill back the other way.

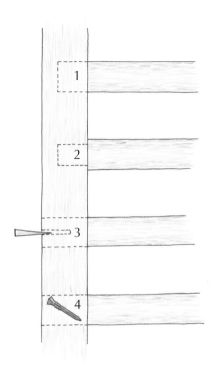

ATTACHING DOWEL

The illustration shows four different methods for attaching a length of dowel to a piece of wood:

1. Drill a hole the same size or slightly smaller than the dowel. Glue the dowel in place.
2. Sharpen the end of the dowel with a knife or file to form a point. Drill a hole large enough for the point. Glue the dowel in place. The clever thing about this method is that the hole is not visible in the final object.
3. Drill a hole right through the piece of wood where you want the dowel to go. Saw a groove in the end of the dowel, insert it into the hole then glue a wedge into the groove. The wedge will have an expanding effect, keeping the dowel securely in place.
4. Drill a hole straight through the piece of wood where you want the dowel to go. Put the dowel in place then hammer a headless pin or nail from the side to fix the dowel.

SCREWS

Screws with a slotted or flat head are rarely used because it is too easy for the screwdriver to skid off the top, although a brass slotted screw head can be a beautiful decorative element. Cross drive screws work well with a screwdriver. Hexhead coach screws and bolts are used for sturdy constructions such as swing frames.

1. Countersunk slotted head screw
2. Roundhead slotted screw
3. Domed head cross drive (Phillips)
4. Trumpet head cross drive PZ
5. Hexhead coach screw
6. Hexhead bolt
7. Carriage bolt

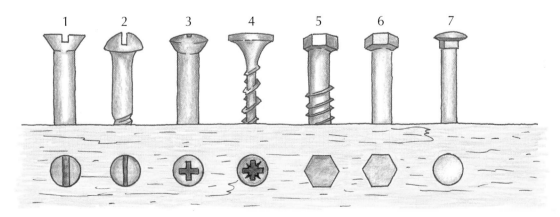

Make your own toolbox

It is good to have a hardwearing box that keeps your basic tools in order. Small items such as drill bits and screws are easily mislaid or lost, and if you have to hunt for a missing hammer or saw before getting going on a project there's a risk you'll give up before you've even started. Have a go at making this easy-but-handy toolbox – you could make a large one for yourself and a smaller one for your little assistant! And if, in the future, the young carpenter loses interest in woodwork, the box can be used for all kinds of things, from collecting pebbles to storing dolls' clothes.

MATERIALS
- 12 mm (½ in) thick sheet plywood
- 25 mm (1 in) dowel
- 15 x 27 mm (½ x 1 in) stripwood
- wood adhesive
- nails and screws

INSTRUCTIONS
Start by drawing the shapes for the two sides, two tall ends and base onto a sheet of plywood and then cut them out using a handsaw or power jig saw. Glue and screw the side and end pieces, then put the bottom piece in place and do the same with it. Cut the stripwood to the right length to fit inside the box. File, saw or drill semicircles in the stripwood to hold small tools (see illustration). Spread adhesive on the ends, place it in position in the box and screw it in place from the outside. Do the same with the handle: cut the dowel to the correct length, put adhesive on the ends and finish by screwing it in place from the outside.

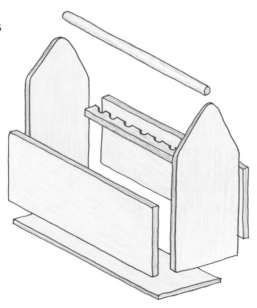

20

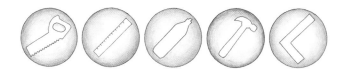

Make your own mitre box

A mitre box is a great help in constructing neat corner joins; for example, when you are making something like a box. Using this comparatively simple device, you can cut the pieces you want to join at a precise angle. When you put them together they will be a perfect fit with no gaps or wrong angles. It isn't especially difficult to make your own mitre box and, as you are the one using it, it doesn't have to look particularly neat. It's a good practice piece to start with: a warm-up for future projects where you might want a better finish. This mitre box will help you make 45° and 90° corners.

Materials
- 1.2 m (4 ft) of 22 x 95 mm (1 x 4 in) planed timber
- wood screws
- wood adhesive

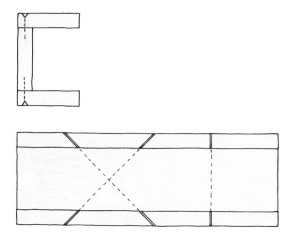

Instructions

Cut the wood into three 40 cm (16 in) lengths. Simply glue and screw these lengths together according to the diagram: one piece for the base and two standing up for the sides. Use a mitre square and pencil on the top to mark the angles. Continue the lines straight down the sides. Then saw a slot down to the bottom following these lines, and your mitre box is ready for use.

When you want to cut something all you have to do is slide the wood into the box and fit the saw into the slot. The slot will ensure the saw doesn't move about or cut at the wrong angle.

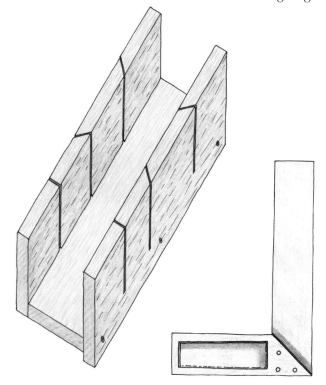

Oil and paint: treating wood surfaces

When treating the surface of wood, bear two things in mind: firstly, you are trying to protect your item (from wear and tear, and from damp), and secondly, you are aiming for a particular look or finish. The kind of surface treatment you choose will depend on whether you want the wood stained or coated, for example. If you want the aging of the wood to show through and feel soft and pleasant to the touch, an oil finish is all that is needed. If you are looking for a more artificial finish, acrylic or spray paint is good as it gives complete cover.

Items that are going to be left outside must be protected from all weathers. They will need a coat of exterior paint, varnish or oil.

Surface treatment options include:

1. **Linseed oil + turpentine.** Mix equal amounts of boiled linseed oil and turpentine. The turpentine helps the wood absorb the oil and dry faster. This is a traditional wood treatment using natural products to give a soft, smooth finish and a beautiful lustre. The treatment doesn't flake and is therefore suitable for exterior wood.

2. **Linseed oil + turpentine + pigment.** You can add a pigment to linseed oil and turpentine to give the finish a lovely colour. This will give you a stain, not a painted finish that completely covers the wood. The wood markings will be seen through the stain but that in itself is a pleasing effect.

3. **Gloss paint.** This is ready-mixed woodwork paint, which you buy in a DIY store. The paint has good coverage properties. Buy water-based gloss so you don't have to use white spirit to clean the brushes. This is the best kind of paint for interior wood.

4. **Spray paint.** Gloss paint in an aerosol spray helps coat surfaces that are hard to reach with a brush. Spray out of doors, preferably, and protect your clothes and other surfaces: spray-paint will inevitably hit surfaces beside and below the item being sprayed.

5. **Acrylic paint.** This is a water-based paint that is synthetically produced and is normally used for painting walls and ceilings. It gives good coverage when used undiluted straight from the tin, or you can mix it with water to produce a stain effect.

First Projects

Small speedy projects are perfect when you want to get started and practise your skills. They are also excellent if you're working with a very young carpenter.

Younger children lose interest quickly and struggle to picture what a complicated construction will look like when it's finished. That's why we have chosen three games and a puzzle to start with. They are quick and simple to make, and adults and children can enjoy them as soon as they are completed, and for years to come.

You can increase the level of difficulty of these projects by making them more detailed and using shapes that are more advanced than the ones we have suggested. Let your imagination run free and create your very own block puzzle with a photograph of the family or of a favourite pet. In the Fox and Sheep game, you can either settle for a red stick as the fox or cut it into the shape of a fox by copying a picture.

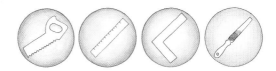

Block jigsaw

It's hard to think of anything easier to make which offers so much fun when completed. You only need nine cubes to make this lovely puzzle to solve alone or together with others. Small children can play with the blocks, while slightly older ones and adults can let the pictures take shape. And because there is no need to join the pieces together or to drill or shape the wood, this is one of the easiest projects in the book.

It's up to you to decide how advanced you want your puzzle to be. The simplest puzzle of all has only one colour on each side. Choosing plain colours helps younger children learn to recognise colours and how to place the blocks side by side to make a whole. They also find it easy to make their own patterns from the different colours.

If you want to increase the level of difficulty you can print out photographs and stick them on the blocks. Coat them with clear varnish afterwards to make them more hard-wearing. You could use family photos from happy events such as birthdays, Christmas or holidays. The child can train his or her memory and learn to differentiate between various events, as well as how to twist and turn the blocks to put the puzzle together. If you can't print out your own pictures you can make a collage by cutting out photos from magazines, or using decorated paper napkins. Or you could paint abstract patterns or lines, or make patterns with rubber stamps to decorate the sides of the blocks.

MATERIALS
- 45 x 45 mm (2 x 2 in) planed timber at least 41 cm (16 in) long
- patterned paper or photos
- paint and brush
- clear varnish

INSTRUCTIONS

Mark and saw the wood into equal-sized cubes. Use a clamp to hold them together in a 3 x 3 grid when you attach your pattern. Glue on a photo, patterned or similar, and wait until it is completely dry before you cut the picture into squares using a sharp knife. When all six sides of each block are finished, paint or spray on a layer of clear varnish.

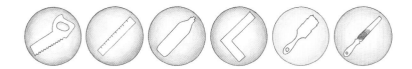

Noughts and Crosses

One version of Noughts and Crosses or Five in a Row is Tic-Tac-Toe. It has a limited play area and the winner of the game is the first player to place three identical pieces in a row. These closely related games date back thousands of years and are believed to have originated in Japan. Over the years various versions with slightly different rules have developed.

The simplest version begins by casting lots to see who starts and who will have which piece. Then each player takes it in turn to move their piece until one player outwits the other and manages to place three of their pieces in a horizontal, vertical or diagonal line.

The base consists of a grid made up of nine squares divided three by three. We have given you a few examples of the different forms your base can take. You might choose a large stable base to use on a table, or a neat little travelling version. You can also draw a grid directly on sand and use shells or pebbles as game pieces, or let the children play with sugar cubes or tooth picks on the checked tablecloths in Italian restaurants – a handy tip for parents who would like to enjoy their coffee in peace!

MATERIALS
- 45 x 45 mm (2 x 2 in) planed timber at least 41 cm (16 in) long
- 19 mm (1 in) thick plywood, 200 x 200 mm (8 x 8 in)
- planed timber and plywood
- dowel of your chosen diameter
- rectangular stripwood

INSTRUCTIONS

Base 1. Follow the directions for the block jigsaw puzzle on page 25 to cut the wood. It's a good idea to use two different kinds of wood or to paint the cubes in two different colours: four in one colour, and five in the other. Join them together using wood adhesive and a clamp. Leave them to dry completely. To protect the base from damp you can apply a couple of layers of clear varnish. The playing pieces are made by sawing three lengths from a piece of dowel and three from a piece of rectangular stripwood. Sand the cut ends lightly and varnish or paint them to make them last longer.

Base 2. Cut a piece of a planed timber of your chosen width to make a rectangle. Then saw a plywood sheet to the same dimensions and measure nine points evenly distributed across the top. Drill out circles and then glue the plywood to the rectangle of wood. With this base you can play with any kind of pieces that fit the holes. The type of finish you choose is up to you. The game will be more durable if the wood is treated in some way (see page 22).

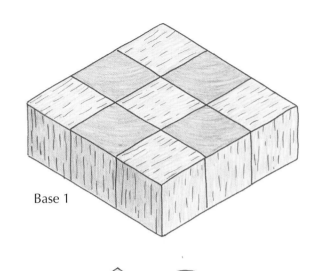

Base 1

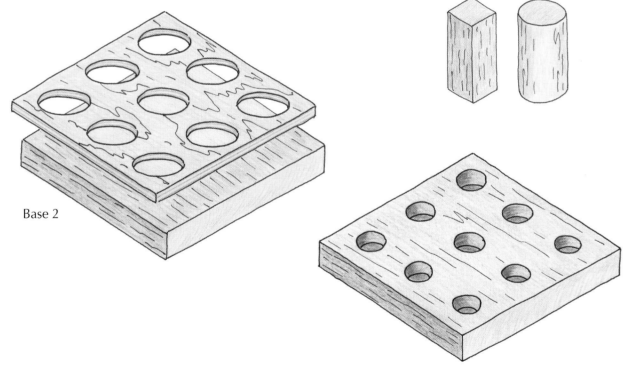

Base 2

27

Fox and Sheep; Solitaire

No special carpentry skills are needed to make this board but it does require careful measuring and a steady hand.

MATERIALS
- planed timber or plywood
- dowel

INSTRUCTIONS
Cut a playing board to the size of your choice. It must be a square and there has to be room for 33 holes, so preferably not smaller than 200 x 200 mm (8 x 8 in). Mark out a grid pattern of eight by eight equal-sized squares. If you have a board that is 200 x 200 mm (8 x 8 in) then each square will be 2½ x 2½ cm (1 x 1 in). Use a mitre square to draw the lines to ensure they are completely straight.

When you have drawn the grid pattern make 33 holes to form a symmetrical cross (see illustration). Mark them with a bradawl or another sharp tool and then drill the holes. It's helpful to remember the tip with the masking tape around the drill bit. You can work out the drilling depth by measuring the thickness of the plank and subtracting half a centimetre. This will ensure you don't drill a hole right through the base.

The playing pieces consist of sawn lengths of dowel of a size that fits into the holes, preferably as snugly as possible. Saw 32 pieces of the same size to play Fox and Sheep or Solitaire, but make a few extra pieces while you are at it. Playing pieces have a tendency to disappear and it's not easy to find replacements afterwards.

Fox and Sheep

The game consists of 20 sheep and two foxes which are painted red. The sheep have to move across the board to the opposite side (where the foxes start).

Toss a coin to find out who will be the foxes and who will be sheep. The foxes always start. They can move in any direction: forwards, backwards, diagonally or sideways. They capture a sheep by jumping over it into an empty hole and the sheep is then taken from the board. The fox can jump several times in one move but can stop wherever it likes.

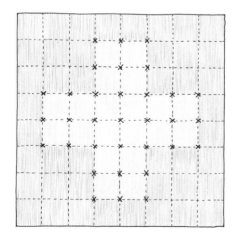

The sheep can move forwards and sideways, but never diagonally or backwards, and they can only ever move one step at a time. They can't capture the fox by jumping over it, but they can trap it in a corner so that it can't go anywhere. When that happens, the sheep have won. The fox wins when it has captured at least twelve sheep.

Solitaire

In this game, just like Fox and Sheep, pieces have to be captured from the board. A single player must think strategically and play so that only one piece remains on the board. It's all about planning your moves so that you jump over the pieces one by one, removing the pieces you have jumped over.

Start by filling 32 of the board's 33 holes, keeping the middle hole empty. This is the starting point of the game. The pieces can move forwards, backwards and sideways, but not diagonally.

The game is over when only one piece is left in the centre hole on the board. You will need to concentrate and think logically to finish this game.

Kubb

You don't need any previous experience to play Kubb. The best thing about this game is that anyone can join in. We have played Kubb with players from two to ninety-two years old. In fact, the two-year-old and the ninety-two-year old played on the same side – and their side won!

You make a Kubb game by sawing kings and soldiers and making throwing batons and field marking pins. If you like you can decorate the kubbs (or blocks) by painting them, adding eyes or anything else you find aesthetically pleasing. You can decorate them as much or as little as you like, although the traditional Kubb components are often left as unadorned wood.

MATERIALS

- 95 x 95mm (4 x 4 in) planed timber, about 30 cm (12 in)
- 70 x 70 mm (3 x 3 in) planed timber, about 1.5 m (5 ft)
- 43 mm (2 in) dowel, about 2 m (6½ ft)
- 15 mm (½ in) dowel, about 2.5 m (8 ft)
- timber for the storage box

INSTRUCTIONS

King: Cut a 30 cm (12 in) length from the thickest piece of wood. Saw a V-shaped cut at the top to look like a crown. Cut out an indentation all the way round to emphasise the shape of the crown. Sand all the surfaces.

Soldiers: Ten soldiers (the kubbs) are formed from the smaller piece of planed timber. Cut it into 15 cm (6 in) lengths. The kubbs don't have to be shaped in any special way, but sand the surfaces so that no-one gets a splinter in their hand.

Throwing batons: Cut the thicker piece of dowel into six pieces of 30 cm (12 in) long. Sand these very carefully to make sure no slivers of wood fly out of them when the players are throwing.

Marking pins: These pins mark out the corners of the pitch and the centre line. The length is not important as long as they can be stuck firmly into the grass with a piece sticking up above ground to show the boundaries. About 35 cm (14 in) would be a suitable length. Cut the thinner dowel into six equal lengths.

Storage box: Make a box from timber you have at home. (Remember that the box must be longer than the longest wooden game piece!) Drill a hole in the centre of each short side and thread a length of cord or rope through and keep it in place with a knot on the outside.

If you want to make the corners extra neat you can use a mitre box to angle the ends of the side pieces, otherwise it is perfectly acceptable to let them overlap, as in the illustration.

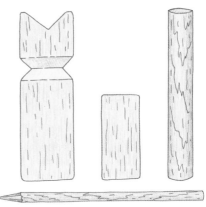

Kubb rules

- Batons can only be thrown underarm and end-over-end. Throwing the baton so that it rotates horizontally is called a helicopter throw and is forbidden.
- Kubbs can only be thrown underarm but are allowed to rotate if the thrower wishes.
- Kubbs are always thrown from the base line (the short end of the pitch).
- Teams take it in turns to throw their three batons towards the kubbs that stand on the opponents' half of the pitch. When all batons have been thrown, it is the other team's turn. The kubbs that have been knocked down are now thrown onto the opposite half of the pitch.
- If the kubb does not come to rest within the opposite half of the pitch after two turns, the other team can stand it anywhere they choose on their pitch half, but not closer than a baton's length from the king's line. The defending team stand up any kubbs that have landed in the correct place.
- The team that threw the kubbs can now throw their batons. The newly thrown kubbs are called field kubbs and they have to be knocked down before the kubbs on the baseline (the base kubbs) can be attacked. When all batons have been thrown play changes hands.

- If a field kubb remains after baton throwing, the team that has the field kubb on its half can stand there and throw instead of standing on the base line. The players stand behind an imagined line running through the kubb, parallel with the base line.
- When one team has knocked down or removed all the kubbs from their opponents' half of the pitch, they are allowed to throw at the king. Throws at the king are always made from the base line.

Note that it is forbidden to topple the king before all the opposing team's kubbs have been knocked down. If anyone happens to knock the king down too early, their team loses the game.

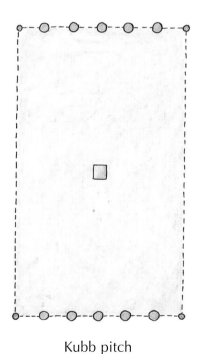

Kubb pitch

Toys

Toys are an important part of a child's development. Children literally play their way into the adult world, and in doing so they learn responsibility and empathy. The odd rule here and there is absorbed at the same time. And, of course, toys are crucial for encouraging imagination and invention.

Toys are thought to have been in existence for as long as human beings. We know for sure that there were toys in ancient Egypt and in ancient Greece. The mass production of toys rapidly increased in the middle of the 1800s and these days there is a huge range to choose from. So why would anyone want to spend a lot of time and energy making their own wooden toys?

Well, as we mentioned at the beginning of the book, it's a question of inspiration, planning, pride and responsibility. It's healthy for people big and small to feel inspired, to plan, make and then use their creation. From the point of view of most children the effort is worth more than money. That's why we want to give you and your little woodworking companion a few tips and ideas for toys that are fun to make and to play with. So get busy sawing … and then get busy playing!

Traffic signs

A safe driver always keeps an eye open for traffic signs warning of speed restrictions, hazards, and so on. To enhance the experience of play and to add an educational slant, you can make a large collection of easily made traffic signs. You can copy existing traffic signs, of course, but you can also make up your own.

Below are examples of some that we have invented, but they have the same function as real signs: stilts on a zebra crossing, parking for hobby horses and a warning for toy tractors. Choose materials and dimensions depending on how large you want the sign to be. Our measurements will be fine for small signs for use on the floor or in the sandpit.

MATERIALS
- 45 x 45 mm (2 x 2 in) planed timber
- 43 mm (2 in) dowel
- 45 mm (2 in) triangular stripwood
- 8 mm (½ in) dowel

INSTRUCTIONS
Saw a piece of wood to make a base. Drill a hole the diameter of the thinner piece of dowel, which will be the pole. Fix the pole in the hole on the base using wood adhesive. Around 10 cm (4 in) is a good length for the pole.

Cut the signs from the thicker piece of dowel or a length of triangular-shaped stripwood. Cut them at least 20 mm (1 in) thick to make them stable enough to sit on the top of the pole. Drill a 10 mm (½ in) diameter hole in the sign where the pole is to be inserted. Brush a little adhesive on the top of the pole and attach the sign. Paint the signs with hobby enamel using a fine brush, or glue on your own printed pictures. To make them really hard-wearing, varnish the signs, poles and bases before using them.

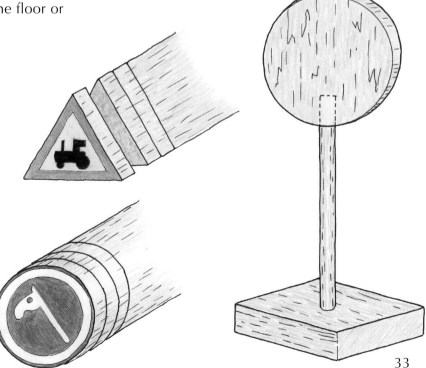

Toy Car

By the time children are one-and-a-half to two years old they can usually make the 'broom broom' sound of a car. And even if there are no toy vehicles available there still seems to be a desire to push something across the floor and make the sound of an engine. On the following pages we give suggestions for different types of four-wheeled vehicles – but why not think up your own model when you have become more proficient? To make simple little cars you need nothing more than an offcut, a piece of stripwood and four wheels.

MATERIALS

- 45 x 95 mm (2 x 4 in) planed timber, about 20 cm (8 in)
- 15 x 15mm (½ x ½ in) stripwood, about 10 cm (4 in)
- 27 mm (1 in) dowel, 4 lengths each 10 cm (4 in) for wheels (or ready-made wheels from a craft shop)

INSTRUCTIONS

Cut the block to your chosen length (the size of the car) and use a pencil to draw the shape of the chassis. The easiest shape can be made by drawing around the bottom of a glass or something similar to make a semicircle. With help, young carpenters can remove the excess wood using a fretsaw, rasp and file. It is easiest to cut away the excess wood using a bandsaw or a jig saw, but naturally that means you must be experienced with such tools, and make sure children are at a safe distance.

Use your imagination when designing your cars, buses, tractors, harvesters, diggers and road rollers. Try to give the various models character. Use a jig saw on solid blocks of wood, or cut out the chassis in plywood and glue the pieces together. You can make a simple bus, for example, from a section of wood 45 x 95 mm (2 x 4 in) or 45 x 120 mm (2 x 5 in). Round off the corners to make the roof and drill shallow holes to make side windows. Attach ready-made wheels or saw slices of dowel for wheels.

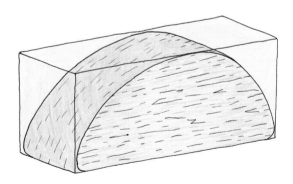

Perhaps the most important thing to remember when you are experimenting with different models is to smooth the surfaces properly with sandpaper so that the vehicles feel safe and comfortable to hold and push about. Not every little chauffeur is careful enough to park their car under cover, so treat the surface if a car or other vehicle is going to be used outdoors. That will protect it from getting damaged when it's left behind in the sandpit and exposed to bad weather.

The illustrations show a few different models. The first resembles a Volkswagen Beetle and the other a Volvo estate with bonnet and hatchback. It will be easier to attach the wheels if you glue two small pieces of stripwood underneath where you want the wheels to be.

Paint the car in your chosen colour, preferably one you have mixed yourself from linseed oil, turpentine and pigment. The wood grain will show through the stain, giving the car a beautiful sheen. Attach black wooden wheels, either bought from a hobby shop or ones you have made yourself by sawing off a slice of dowel. Use slotted roundhead screws. Drill a hole in the centre of the wheel. The hole should be slightly wider than the screw. Place a wooden washer between the wheel and the wood it is going to be attached to. Attach the screw to the stripwood, making a hole first with a smaller drill bit to make sure the wood doesn't split. The screw must sit firmly in the wood and rotate in the wheel.

Ready, steady, drive!

Tractor

MATERIALS

- 45 x 120 mm (2 x 5 in) planed timber, about 20 cm (8 in)
- 12 x 12 mm (½ x ½ in) stripwood
- 10 or 12 mm (½ in) thick sheet plywood
- 10 mm (½ in) dowel
- 2 large back wheels
- 2 smaller front wheels

INSTRUCTIONS

Begin by sawing the basic shape (the chassis) from the stripwood. Then draw the side cab panels on to plywood and cut them out. Sand the edges with fine sandpaper. Glue the panels to the base and hold them in place with a clamp until the adhesive has dried. Measure the size of the roof and saw a suitable piece from plywood. Glue the roof over the gap between the side panels.

Measure the width of the base and cut two lengths of stripwood. These will be the axles. Glue them to the underside of the base a suitable distance apart and pre-drill a hole at each end so that the wood does not split when you screw on the wheels later. Place a metal washer between the wheel and end of the axle when you attach the wheel to make it turn more easily. Finish by adding an exhaust stack pipe by cutting off a suitable length of dowel diagonally at one end. Drill a hole in the bonnet section and glue the dowel in place. Apply a surface finish if the tractor is intended for outdoor use.

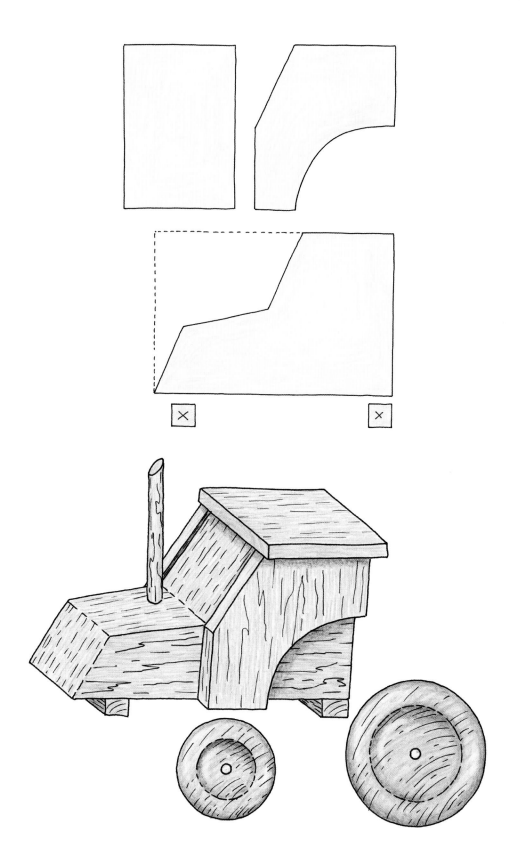

Boat

Many of us will remember a fascination with the sea and boats when we were very young. It certainly is fun to watch passenger ships as big as tower blocks or enormous cargo freighters come alongside to dock, or turn into narrow harbours with the utmost precision.

Our toy boat is not designed to go to sea, but with a bit of imagination it is not difficult to build harbours and quays in the sandpit, or indoors on a blue blanket or sheet. Boats are among the easiest toys to make. With a flat bottom and no revolving wheels to attach, you can focus instead on deck details such as the railings, funnels, wheelhouse and cabins. Saw the hull pieces from a piece of planed timber and use blocks and dowel for making the deck fittings.

INSTRUCTIONS

With offcuts from previous projects you will at least be able to make a simple dinghy. Our fishing boat is about 20 cm (8 in) long and the hull is made from a piece of 45 x 90 mm (2 x 4 in) planed timber.

Saw a pointed end to form the boat's bow and round off the other end to form the stern. Attach a small block of your chosen size on the rear end of the deck towards the stern, and a thin piece of dowel beside it. This will be the wheelhouse and the stack. Place a slightly longer piece of dowel closer towards the bow to give the boat a mast.

You can also add finishing touches to the deck, such as hatches. Paint and then treat the surface as desired, depending on personal choice. The paint should be finished with a good layer of varnish, just like a real wooden boat.

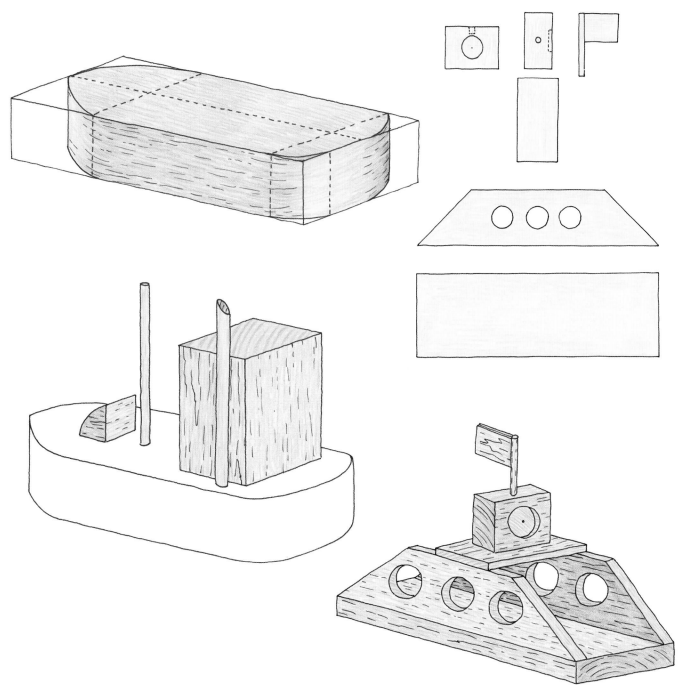

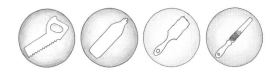

Hobby horse

A hobby horse is a fun method of transport for a little rider. For centuries children have enjoyed this popular and ingenious toy.

MATERIALS

- 12 mm (½ in) thick sheet plywood
- 22 x 45 mm (1 x 2 in) batten, about 1.25 m (4 ft)
- 60 mm (2 in) wooden wheel
- pen
- wood adhesive
- screws
- nuts
- hobby enamel or acrylic
- paint
- string

INSTRUCTIONS

Cut one end of the batten diagonally to represent an ear. (If you like, you can attach a wooden wheel at the other end to protect the floor. In that case, use a screw and nut so the wheel can rotate.) Draw the outline of a horse's head about 30 cm (12 in) long on to plywood and cut it out. The head is held in place with glue and two screws in the neck. Drill a hole through the muzzle and thread string through for reins.

Graph paper is a simple way to enlarge a small image. Draw a grid pattern on a small picture or use the template on page 41. Then draw larger squares on a piece of cardboard or directly onto the sheet of plywood. Draw the outline of the smaller picture using the grid lines as a guide.

Cut a slot in one end of a length of thick dowel. Insert the head into the slot and fasten it with glue and screws.

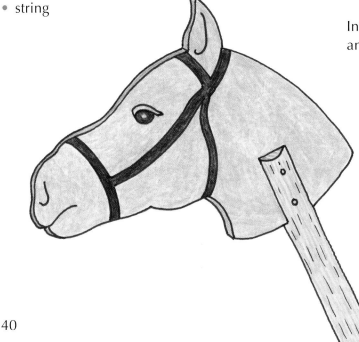

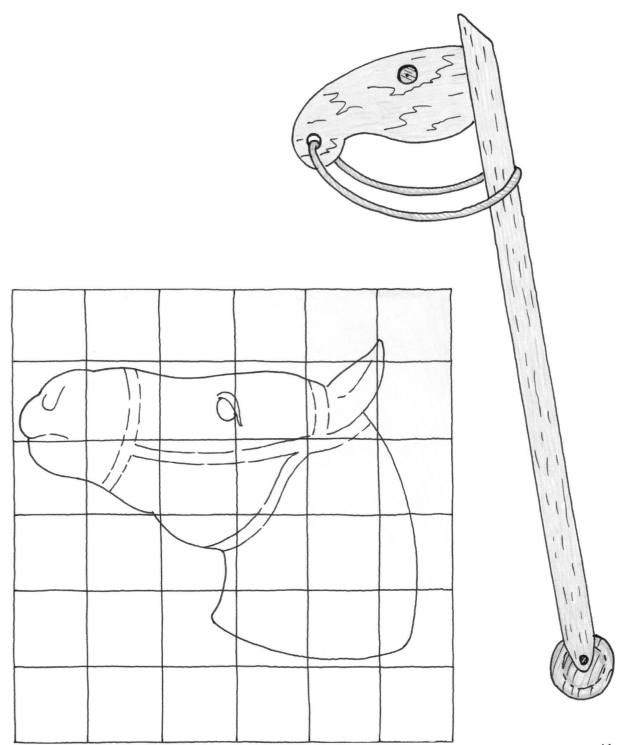

Sword

Dressing up as historical figures such as knights, Vikings, or pirates is a popular game for children from about three to quite a bit older. Often adults can be seen joining in the games, and it's much more fun if everyone has accessories to make the play seem more realistic. That's why it is a good idea to make several swords. They can be based on authentic designs or made into weird and wonderful shapes from your own imagination.

Swords are weapons, so we feel it's a good idea to somehow signify that these are toys. If you make a knight's sword as illustrated here, you can paint it in a colour not associated with real swords, or decorate it with a pattern of some kind. The grey sword illustrated here would undoubtedly look much more friendly if it had flowers painted on the shaft. And if lots of children are involved in the game it is a good idea to have an adult standing by to stop the game getting too wild, as even a sword made of wood can cause damage to someone's face or body.

Our swords are intended to be attractive details to add to a costume, fearlessly thrust into a belt as the little knights gallop off on their hobby horses.

MATERIALS
- 12 mm (½ in) thick sheet plywood
- a piece of stripwood

INSTRUCTIONS
The easiest way is to saw your chosen design from a template or freehand from a sheet of plywood. Avoid chipboard because it breaks too easily. Glue and screw on a couple of short pieces of stripwood (see illustration) as a handle. File and sand it to make it easy to hold.

You can make a more elaborate sword from a piece of batten. Draw a suitable shape and cut out the whole sword, including the handle, in one piece. Then saw a hilt, which you attach with glue after sawing indentations in both the sword and the hilt. You can also choose to saw the hilt from the same piece as the rest of the sword.

Shield

A dressing-up costume with a sword should have a stylish, protective shield to go with it. The construction of a shield is fairly straightforward, as it is basically a large flat surface. Here, we show you four simple but appealing shapes and patterns. If you want to put more imagination into the shields you can of course paint more detailed patterns. That would also make them decorative enough to hang on a wall when not being used in a game. Why hide such pieces of art away in a cupboard?

MATERIALS

- 10 mm (½ in) thick plywood, about 50 x 50 cm (20 x 20 in)
- 12 mm (½ in) dowel
- 22 x 45 mm (1 x 2 in) stripwood, about 10 cm (4 in)
- a strip of leather or a piece of an old belt
- pen
- screws
- hobby enamel or acrylic paint

INSTRUCTIONS

A clever way to make sure your shield has symmetrical halves is to first draw the outline on paper and then transfer it onto the sheet of plywood. Fold the paper in half, draw your chosen outline, cut round it (still with the paper folded), and then open it out. You are sure to be familiar with this technique from cutting out perfectly symmetrical heart shapes.

Use your paper template to draw the shape on the plywood. Read more about enlarging an image using graph paper or a grid on page 41. You will find cutting the plywood is faster using a jig saw, if you have access to one, but a hand-held saw is just as good.

Make the handle by attaching the dowel to a small block at each end so that you can thread your fingers between the dowel and the shield. You can also mount a leather band at a suitable distance from the dowel. This will help to hold the upper arm in place against the shield. Attach the leather band with tacks. Remember that it has to sit loosely enough for a small arm to get behind it. Decorate the shield as you choose.

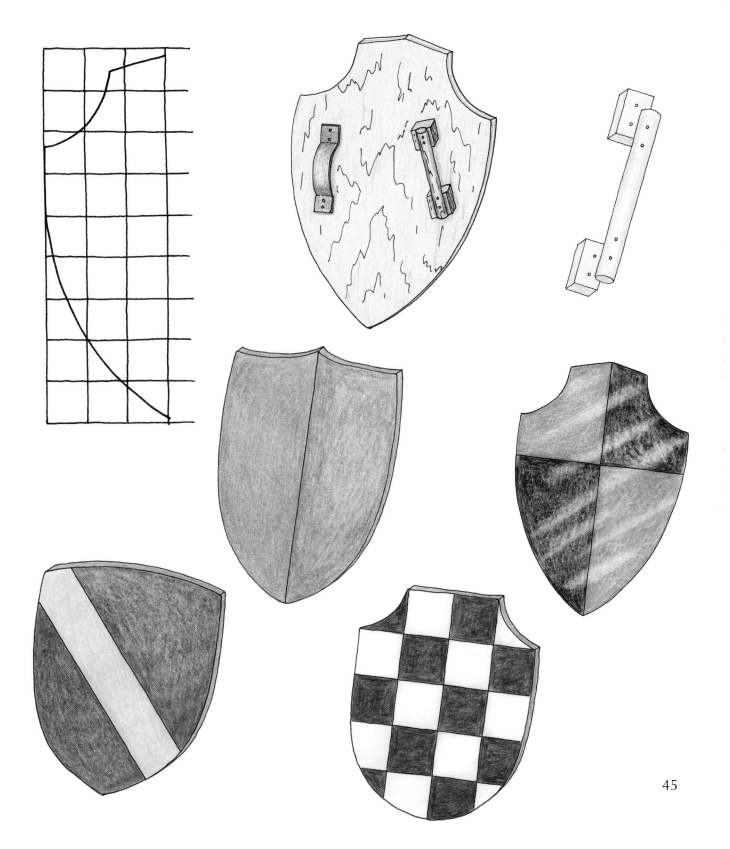

45

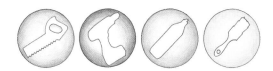

Electric guitar

Every guitar hero wants to own a guitar to look after and love. Here we offer a few inspirational suggestions for making your own unique guitar by playing with different designs and colours.

MATERIALS

- 12 mm (½ in) thick sheet plywood, about 50 x 50 cm (20 x 20 in)
- 22 x 70 mm (½ x 3 in) planed timber, about 50 cm (20 in)
- 10 mm (½ in) dowel, about 20 cm (8 in)
- 25 mm (1 in) dowel, about 5 cm (2 in)
- wooden or polystyrene ball
- pen
- wood adhesive
- screws
- hobby enamel or acrylic paint

INSTRUCTIONS

First make a sketch on a piece of paper of what you want your guitar to look like. Don't be afraid to go let yourself go – most designs are possible. Draw your design in your chosen size – about 30 cm (12 in) for smaller children – on a sheet of plywood. An electric jig saw will make cutting out easier.

Saw the neck of the guitar, about 40 cm (16 in) long, from planed timber or from plywood, and then glue and screw it to the guitar body. The very simplest guitar consists of a body and a neck. Additional details such as tuning pegs, volume knobs, strings and so on are not difficult to achieve.

You can make a tremolo arm from a piece of dowel with a ball glued to one end. Shave the other end so that it lies flat against the guitar body. The volume knobs are cut from thicker

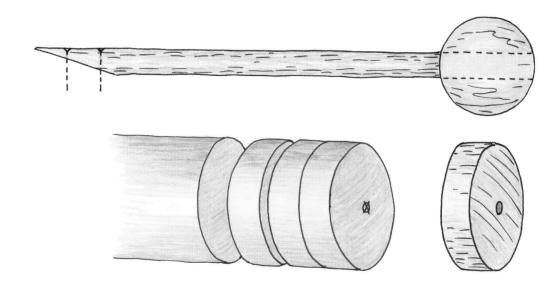

dowel. Attach them to the guitar body with glue or screws. If you decide to screw them on, make a small hole first, otherwise they might split.

Buy transfers, stars or other glittery details and stick them on. It's best to finish with a coat of clear varnish if you want the decorations to survive lots of riffs and gigs. You can create exciting colour combinations with hobby enamel or acrylic paint. It will look neater if you varnish or paint the various parts before you attach them.

Play Equipment

Fresh air is good for you – hardly anyone would disagree with that. Areas designed for playing outdoors should encourage children to have fun, which in turn generates a desire to be outside. That's why we think it's important to include a few projects showing how to create an attractive outdoor environment.

The advantage of making wooden outdoor toys is that they are often sturdy, durable products that last for years, perhaps even several generations, or at least for one generation of siblings. In other words, none of these larger projects are designed to be made on the spur of the moment. If you do a proper job from the beginning your creation will last longer. You might need to maintain it by giving it a clean or some protection, but apart from that nothing more should need to be done. Swing frames, slides and sandpits are examples of play-friendly projects adapted for children, and here we give you some suggestions of what such building projects can look like. Stilts are fun to play with outdoors as well as inside, and they are quick and fairly easy to make. Whether it's easy to walk on them is another matter, and a certain amount of practice is definitely required. It's always amusing when children realise they are better at walking on them than adults. It's an activity that makes people laugh, both old and young. So, take a few deep breaths of fresh air – and get started.

Pirate ship

This pirate ship is ideal for games of Shipwreck, or Don't Touch the Ground, as it is also known. Lay out a route of cushions or chairs with the wheel and flagpole at either end. Make your way along it without touching the ground – no matter how rough the weather!

MATERIALS

- 45 x 70 mm (2 x 3 in) pressure-treated timber, size depending on dimensions and number of sections
- 22 x 95 mm (1 x 4 in) planed timber, size depending on dimensions and number of sections
- 45 x 45 mm (2 x 2 in) planed timber, about 150 cm (5 ft)
- 25 mm (1 in) dowel, about 1.6 m (5 ½ ft)
- 70 x 70 mm (3 x 3 in) plywood
- pen
- screws
- wood oil or exterior paint
- for wood

INSTRUCTIONS

Our ship has a frame of pressure-treated timber because it will be standing on the ground. The floor is made of planed timber planks which are lightly sanded to give a soft and splinter-free surface. We have used plywood and dowel for the ship's wheel and the flagpole. The wheel is permanently fixed to the front of the bow (see illustration).

There are fore and aft sections. You can easily elongate the ship by building more plinths with flooring to jump on to. In that case, they will form the middle sections of the ship and can consist of anything from one to perhaps ten parts. Place them about one metre (3 ft) apart to make a really big, exciting ship.

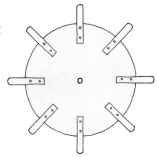

Swing frame

A swing frame can be very simple and won't take up too much room if you build crossed supports and a cross bar with room for one swing. If you want to expand the concept, it's easy to allow room for more swings or perhaps add a little platform or a climbing section. All you have to do is make two diagonal cross supports or A-frames, then anchor them in the ground at your preferred distance apart. Our illustration shows the proportions for a frame with room for two swings, or perhaps one swing and one climbing rope, as well as a small wooden platform to climb up to. You could also build walls below the platform to create a cosy little house or den.

MATERIALS

- 45 x 145 mm (2 x 6 in) pressure-treated timber, about 12 m (40 ft)
- 95 x 95 mm (4 x 4 in) rough sawn timber or pressure-treated planed timber, about 4 m (13 ft)
- angle brackets
- carriage bolts, washers and lock nuts

INSTRUCTIONS

To build the basic frame with crossed supports and a cross bar, make three diagonal crosses from pressure-treated timber. Make each part 2.9 m (10 ft) long and hold them together with a carriage bolt, washer and lock nut.

The cross bar which will hold the swings could consist of rough sawn timber or a piece of planed timber. Calculate the length of the cross bar depending on how many swings, ropes or ladders you want to have. Ours is 3.4 m (11 ft) and has room for one swing, one rope and one ladder, and a platform for a slide. Use angle brackets to attach the cross bar to the upright supports, so it will be easy to dismantle the frame when it has served its purpose. Screw the brackets into the wood (nails have a tendency to work themselves out as the frame moves).

Dig holes to anchor the upright supports firmly in the ground so that the frame does not tip over. Cover the ground below the frame with sand to give it a soft surface.

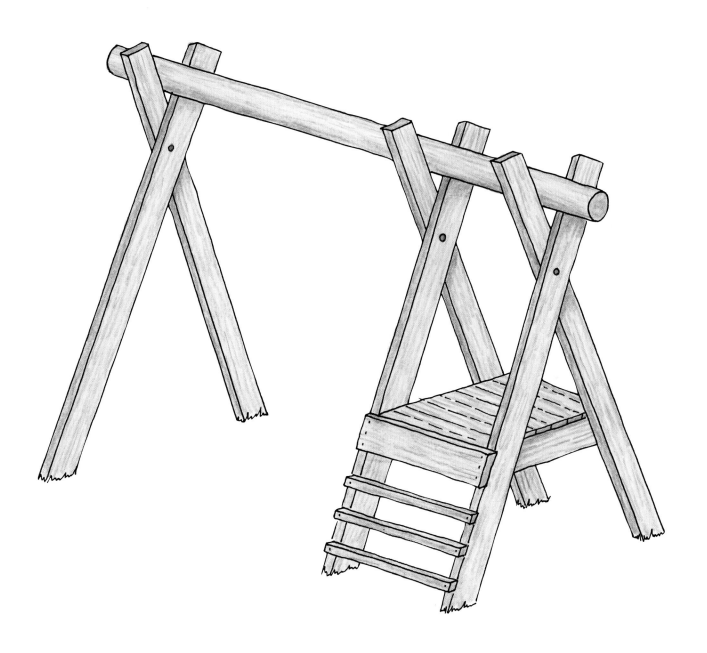

Wooden swing

If there is not enough room in your garden or outdoor play area to build a large swing frame, you might still have somewhere suitable to hang a swing. It could be a nearby tree perhaps, or two fixed points such as a garage or outbuilding between which you can attach a sturdy length of timber as a cross bar. Naturally, it is extremely important to check the strength of the branch or garage wall to make sure the swing does not come loose. Choose a really thick branch if you are going to hang the swing in a tree and make sure the branch is not rotten.

We have made a classic wooden swing consisting of nothing more than a couple of seat boards and the means for hanging them up. To make it more comfortable to sit on, and easier to balance, we have chosen to fix an angled base block at each end and lay two boards across them. The boards slope in towards the middle, making a slight hollow to sit in. That way, the child using the swing will feel more secure.

MATERIALS
- 45 x 70 mm (2 x 3 in) planed timber, 2 pieces each 22 cm (9 in)
- 22 x 120 mm (1 x 5 in) planed timber, 2 pieces each 47 cm (18 in)
- rust-free screws

INSTRUCTIONS
When you have assembled the two blocks and the two seat boards, screw them in place from underneath. Drill two holes through the short ends, one at each corner, slightly in from the edge. Thread rope through the holes. Towing rope used for small boats, for example, is durable and hardwearing. Tie both ropes around the cross bar or tree using a clove hitch. Remember not to tie the rope too tight – it must be able to glide backwards and forwards a little when someone is swinging. Feel the sense of freedom and the wind in your hair!

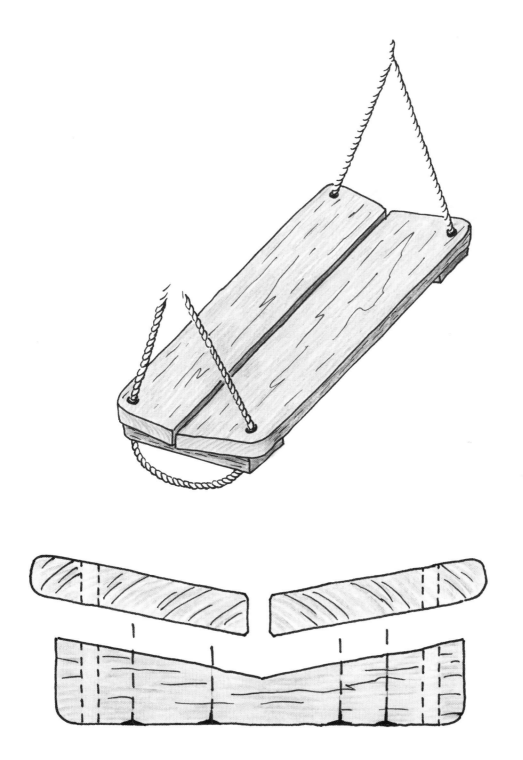

Climbing frame

After you have made a few things you might feel confident enough to integrate a swing into a climbing frame, or build a beautiful climbing frame to stand on its own in the garden. This project is designed for those who already have some experience. You can start with the model illustrated opposite, but why not experiment with different platforms and levels in various colours? Just remember to clear away any stones or rocks when you have decided where to position your climbing frame. Ideally, build it on soft sand, in case there is an accident and a little climber takes a tumble. It's also wise not to build it too tall; it's better to make interesting extensions sideways instead of upwards.

MATERIALS
• planed timber, pressure-treated timber, treated plywood, depending on design

INSTRUCTIONS
Dig four holes and anchor the corner posts to cover an area of just over a square metre. It is best to use 95 x 95 mm (4 x 4 in) pressure-treated timber to prevent damp creeping into the wood and making it rot. Treated timber should not be painted immediately, so if you want to paint it you must wait at least a year. Build a frame around the posts to give the climbing frame extra stability. When you have finished constructing your tower you can fit a piece of geotextile inside the frame at the bottom and then pour a layer of sand on top to create a snug little sandpit with a roof.

Nail a second frame around the corner posts, about one metre (3 ft) up. Construct the frame from 45 x 95mm (2 x 4 in) planed timber, about a metre (3 ft) long. Fit a floor inside the frame.

Attach a balcony rail on two sides, half a metre (1½ ft) up from the floor, and fill it in with planks. This will provide a safe place out of the wind to sit and play. Give the climbing frame a tower made of waterproof material or treated plywood so that it can withstand the wet by covering it with rainproof material or bitumen.

The simplest roof consists of a single sloping sheet: a so-called shed roof. To make a more advanced roof construction build two A-shaped roof trusses and attach two sheets of plywood to resemble a normal house roof (also known as a pitched roof). The church tower shown on the large illustration is called a hip roof or a pyramidal roof. The basic principle is to construct two A-frames and prop them against each other to give four faces and a point at the top.

Stilts

Stilts are quick to make: our model should only take about an hour. On the other hand, it takes more than an hour to learn to walk on them properly, but perseverance pays off and if you don't give up you will certainly become an expert before long. The very youngest should not attempt it but children from about five years old can have lots of fun with stilts. Watching is not as much fun, so it's a good idea to have a couple of extra pairs to bring out when friends come to visit.

MATERIALS

- 45 x 45 mm (2 x 2 in) planed timber, 2 pieces each 2 m (6 ft)
- 45 x 95 mm (2 x 4 in) planed timber, 70 cm (2 ft)

INSTRUCTIONS

Cut the shorter length of timber diagonally into four sections following the diagram so that each section measures 25 cm (10 in) on one side and 10 cm (4 in) on the opposite side. Glue and screw them to the long pieces of wood. You can decide how high up you want them to be. Use countersunk round headscrews – as long as possible – to make the foot supports stable and durable. Approximately 12 cm (5 in) long screws work well, as long as they don't go right through the wood. It's a good idea to treat the wood with oil and turpentine containing a little pigment to give the stilts colour and sheen.

If you want to make rather more advanced and intricate foot supports you can use the two models illustrated opposite as a guide. Off you go!

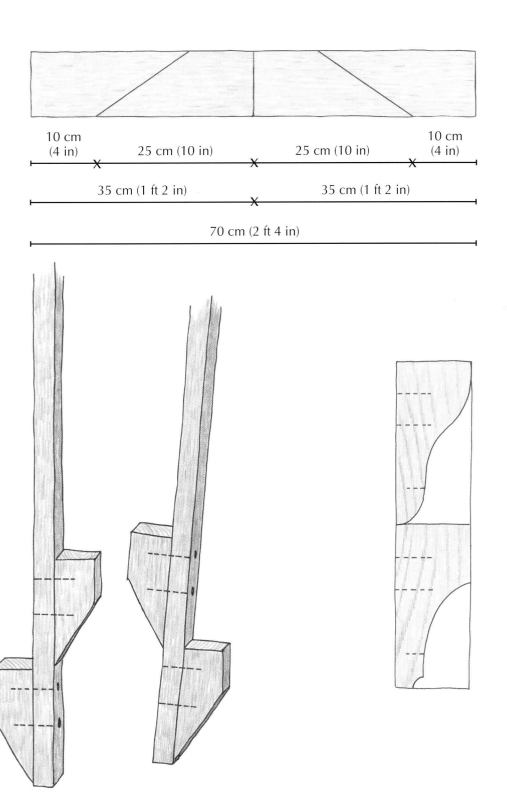

10 cm
(4 in)

25 cm (10 in)

25 cm (10 in)

10 cm
(4 in)

35 cm (1 ft 2 in)

35 cm (1 ft 2 in)

70 cm (2 ft 4 in)

Sandpit

It's easy to have fun and be inventive when playing in a sandpit. A young architect can build an entire community, while a young artist can create sculptural hills and valleys.

A well-built sandpit can last for many years, especially if you treat it with wood oil, for example. It's well worth doing because even older children like to build sandcastles.

MATERIALS
- 45 x 120 mm (2 x 5 in) planed timber, about 12 m (40 ft)
- 22 x 160 mm (1 x 6 in) planed timber, about 7 m (23ft)
- 45 x 70 mm (2 x 3 in) planed timber, about 1 m (3 ft)
- wood oil
- geotextile
- sandpit sand

INSTRUCTIONS
Dig a shallow hole in the ground where the sandpit will be, or place it level on the ground; either way will do. It won't really matter how high you make the surrounding edge, as long as children can climb in and out easily. A simple frame of rough-hewn planks or beams joined together with angle brackets and with a base of geotextile will be perfectly adequate. You can make a slightly more advanced model by joining the corners together using small blocks of wood.

A flat rim to sit on will make the sandpit more comfortable for adults who want to join in the play. Sand the surface to avoid any risk of splinters for small or big people.

Making interesting and exciting sandpits is very easy, even without getting involved in any carpentry. An old worn-out wooden dinghy, for example, makes a wonderful sandpit, should you have the chance to get hold of one. Tractor tyres filled with sand are also lots of fun, and if you have several you can place them in a group and paint them bright colours.

You can buy play sand in sacks from building merchants or garden centres. If you are going to need a lot it might be worth hiring a trailer and buying in bulk.

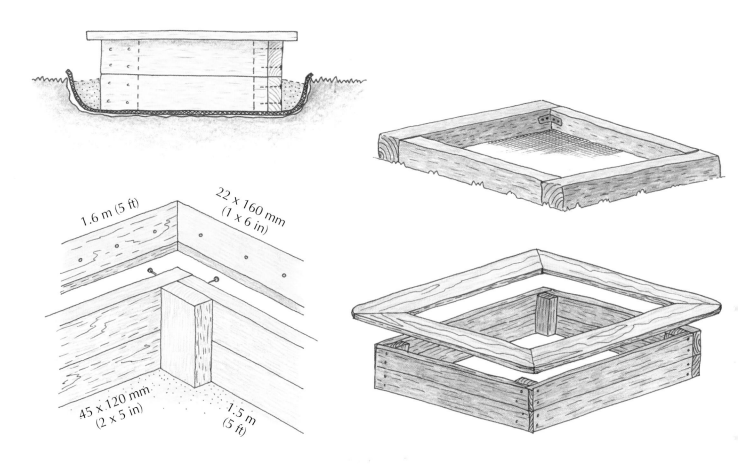

1.6 m (5 ft)

22 x 160 mm
(1 x 6 in)

45 x 120 mm
(2 x 5 in)

1.5 m
(5 ft)

House and Garden

There are lots of interesting, simple and practical projects to make everyday routines easier for little people and their parents.

It doesn't take long to make a wooden boot jack and a shoe scraper, or an ingenious coat stand at a suitable height for children. Or what about a decorative clothes ladder? We'll also give tips on how to make a staircase safe for children so they don't tumble through the banisters and down the stairs. These are simple adaptations to your home, which can easily be reversed when the children have grown and the risk of hurting themselves on the stairs has passed.

Providing birds with food during the winter is a kind gesture, and in this chapter we also show you how to make an unusual arrangement for feeding them. Place it outside your kitchen window and you can eat at the same time as the birds. You can also build an exciting bird's nest in a multi-storey design and with a little luck attract more nesting families to your garden during spring.

Shoe scraper

This traditional shoe scraper is smart, practical and quite simple to make. Naturally, its length varies, depending on the amount of room in your doorway and the number of people who will be using it at the same time.

MATERIALS

- 28 x 28 mm (1 x 1 in) stripwood, 6 pieces of 80 or 120 cm (2 or 3 ft)
- 45 x 70 mm (2 x 3 in) pressure-treated planed timber, 3 pieces
- rust-free screws

INSTRUCTIONS

Use three or four supports and cut out V-shaped notches as shown in the illustration. Attach the scraper bars from underneath using rust-free screws. Make sure you buy knot-free, close-grained timber. If heavy adults are going to use the scraper, the dimensions should be increased from 28 x 28 mm (1 x 1 in) to 35 x 35 mm (1½ x 1½ in) for added strength. Apply several good layers of wood oil to the finished shoe scraper.

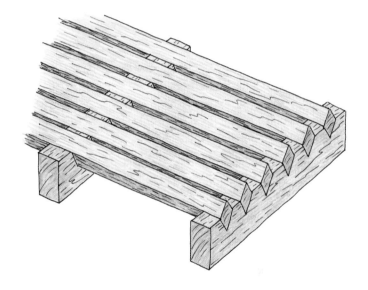

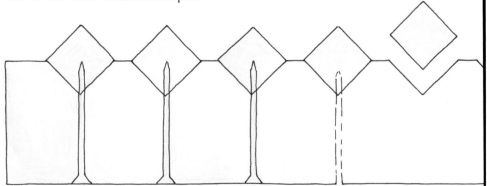

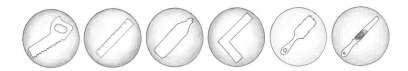

Boot jack

Muddy boots are horrible to handle when you have been out in wet weather. They also seem to have a tendency to stick to your feet, making them difficult to take off. If you use a boot jack you won't have to grab hold of a muddy boot. By placing your heel in the notch, resting the other foot on the jack and then pulling your foot out of the boot, the problem is solved. The principle is simple and a boot jack can be used by very young children. When the jack is too large it causes a problem for very small users who have difficulty keeping their balance, so a good tip is to make the jack in several different sizes.

MATERIALS
- 45 x 45 mm (2 x 2 in) planed timber
- 22 x 120 mm (1 x 5 in) planed timber
- countersunk round head screws

INSTRUCTIONS
By far the easiest and quickest model is the blue boot jack (below). A V-shaped notch has been cut out of the timber and a block about 5 cm (2 in) high has been screwed to the bottom. Where the block is attached, it is cut at an angle so that the jack will slope without wobbling. The second illustration shows how you can develop the simplest model into a more stylish and comfortable version. Saw a U-shaped groove for the boot and cut both the underneath of the block and the end of the timber (the bit where you press with the other foot) at an angle to make a really stable, non-tip boot jack.

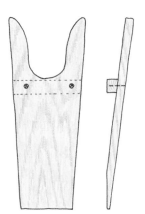

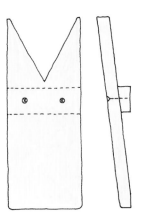

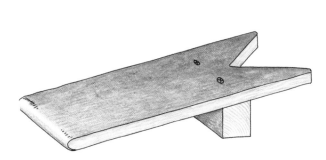

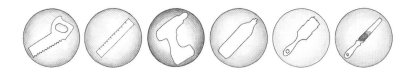

Boot rack

A boot rack will keep all your boots tidy and give them a chance to dry inside and out. This is a wall-mounted rack – ideally it should be attached above a radiator, but at a fairly low level to make it easy to reach. All you have to do is calculate the number of boots you want on each rack: lots of pairs will naturally require a longer rack.

MATERIALS

- 45 x 90 mm (2 x 3 in) planed timber
- 21 mm (1 in) dowel, 2 for each boot pair
- screws
- wood adhesive

INSTRUCTIONS

Drill indentations for the dowels which will support the boots. Use a suitably sized drill bit so you can just about fit the dowel into the hole without any gaps. It's best to add a drop of wood adhesive to the hole to help the dowel stay in place. Choose the length of the dowel depending on the size of the boots – a few shorter ones for children and longer ones for adults. Finish it off with oil or varnish, or a coat of paint. Choose the finish depending on what suits your hall or utility room. Screw the boot rack straight on to the wall or on the side of a cupboard, using the right kind of screws and rawlplugs for the surface.

Clothes ladder

A clothes ladder is another practical storage item. It can be used for clothes you don't want to hang in the wardrobe because they have been worn but are not quite ready for the laundry basket. The clothes ladder is also practical if you are the organised type who likes to get clothes ready for the next day. A clothes ladder can be narrow or wide, tall or short. Find a place where you would like it to stand and adapt it to the space available. Our ladder is fairly tall and the rungs are placed at 45 cm (1½ ft) intervals. The width of the ladder is also 45 cm (1½ ft).

MATERIALS
- 28 x 70 mm (1 x 3 in) planed timber, 2 pieces about 2 m (7 ft)
- 25 mm (1 in) dowel
- wood adhesive
- clear varnish

INSTRUCTIONS
Lean one piece of timber against the wall. The lower end should be about 50–60 cm (2 ft) away from the wall. Put an upright wooden block on the floor right next to this. Draw a line on the timber, using the block as a marker. The line must be parallel to the floor and wall respectively. Do the same with the upper edge, this time holding the block against the wall. Saw along the lines.

There are various ways of fastening the dowel rungs to the uprights. They all work the same way, so choose the one you like best. Various options are below.

1. Drill halfway through an upright, marking the drill bit before you start to avoid drilling right through the wood. Put a drop of adhesive in the hole and insert the dowel.
2. Saw a line around the dowel and carve away about ½ cm (¼ in) around the dowel with a knife. Drill a sufficiently large hole in the upright and fix the dowel in the hole with wood adhesive as above.
3. Saw a horizontal groove in both ends of the dowel and drill through the upright. Carve a small wooden wedge and knock it into the dowel as far as it will go. If the wedge protrudes from the upright all you have to do is cut it off at the same level with a fine saw such as a Japanese trim saw.
4. The easiest way: drill right through the upright and insert the dowel. Keep it in place with adhesive and a nail which you knock in from the side.

Paint or decorate your ladder by glueing on pictures or scraps with wallpaper paste. Finish with a layer of clear varnish.

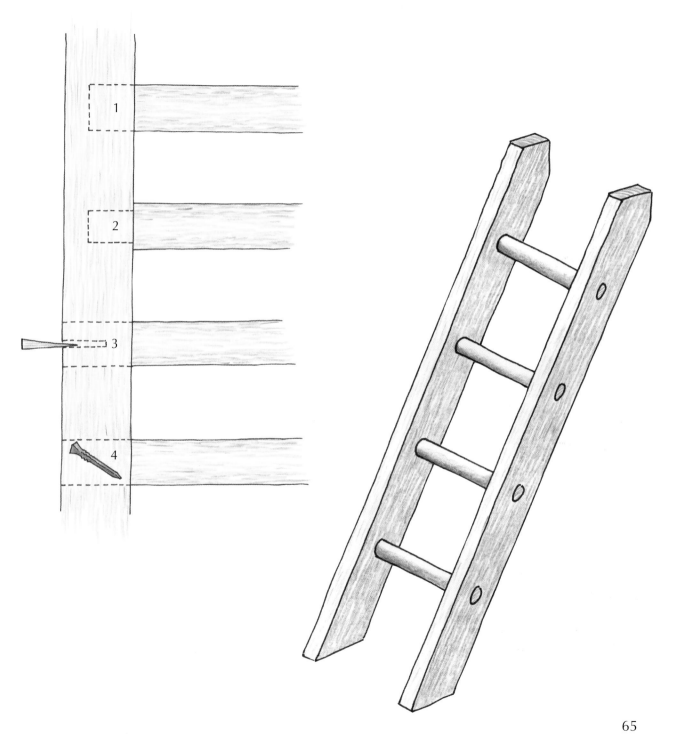

Coat stand

A free-standing coat stand can be very useful. You probably already have wall-mounted hooks for children's clothes, but with our version you have a mobile addition that can be tidied away if you don't want it on view. Our coat stand is adapted to suit young children so that they can hang up their clothes themselves. If you like, you can make the stand taller and add more pegs.

MATERIALS
- 45 x 45 mm (2 x 2 in) planed timber,
- 4 pieces, each 1.2 m (4ft)
- 45 x 90 mm (2 x 4 in) planed timber, 2 pieces, each 40 cm (16 in)
- 12 mm (½ in) dowel, 4 pieces, each 25 cm (10 in)
- 8 wooden balls

INSTRUCTIONS
Saw a slot 45 x 45 mm (2 x 2 in) in the centre of each of the two short pieces of timber. Fit them together to make a cross. Screw and glue the four upright posts into each corner of the cross. Drill right through the four uprights 12 cm (5 in) from the top of the stand. Make the hole as big as (or marginally bigger than) the diameter of the dowel, about 12 cm (5 in).

Turn the coat stand a quarter turn and drill through all the uprights slightly higher up, this time about 8 cm (3 in) from the top. Place a piece of wood in the space between the uprights to make drilling easier: it stabilises the uprights while you drill.

Hammer or push in the dowel to form the pegs. Make sure there is the same distance between the uprights at the base and the top of the stand. Often when the dowel is inserted the uprights move slightly and distort the construction, so that needs to be avoided.

On our coat stand we have allowed the dowel to protrude the same distance in all directions, but for a more dynamic design you could make them stick out at different lengths. It can actually be more practical if the coats don't hang against each other, especially if it has been raining.

Finish by glueing a wooden ball on the end of each peg. Sand all the edges and corners. Let the coat stand keep its natural wood finish or experiment with colour. Make sure the surface is completely dry before you start using the stand.

If you would like a more intricate foot you can round off the corners. The illustration opposite gives some simple, aesthetically pleasing examples.

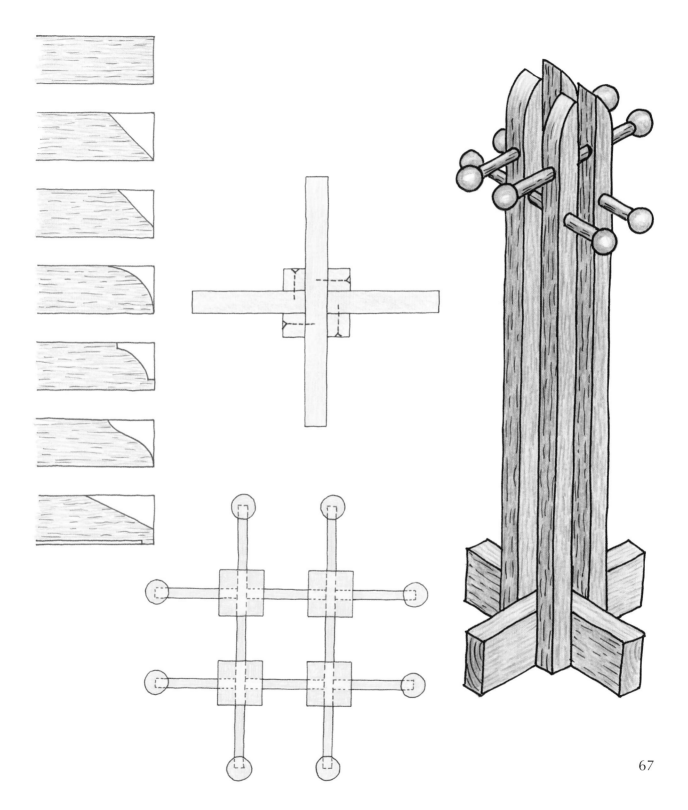

Bird feeder

This bird feeder is a nice decorative feature to have outside the kitchen window. It offers a feast for small birds and you can make a banquet for them from all sorts of food. The idea is to hang or spear the food on the lengths of dowel that stick out from the centre post. The dowel is sharpened to make it easy to thread on fruit and other things, which is why it's important to have the post high enough so that children won't run into it and hurt themselves. Obviously, the food is intended for birds; to keep cats, dogs and foxes away it is good to have a tall post out of reach of our four-legged friends.

If you prefer, you can insert sticks with indentations, rather than sharp sticks. You can then hang fat balls and other delicious things for the birds, without the food falling off and making a mess. Be prepared to put your bird feeder out before the temperature drops below zero: if the ground freezes you will not be able to fix it deeply enough for it to stay upright all winter.

MATERIALS
- 45 x 45 mm (2 x 2 in) planed timber, 2 m (7 ft)
- 12 mm (½ in) dowel, 1 m
- 12 mm (½ in) drill bit
- wood adhesive for outdoor use

INSTRUCTIONS

Plane the timber to make it eight-sided, with each side about 18 mm (1 in) wide. If you want to make it easier to sink the feeder into the ground, you can make a point at one end with an axe. Then drill holes approximately 10 mm (½ in) deep for the dowel to sit in. Space them evenly around the eight sides at different heights so they are not too close together. Fix the dowel in place with adhesive and treat the surface with oil, varnish or exterior paint. A good tip to make the project a little easier and faster, especially if you don't have a plane, is to buy eight-sided pressure-treated posts of various heights. They are not especially expensive and are very easy to work with.

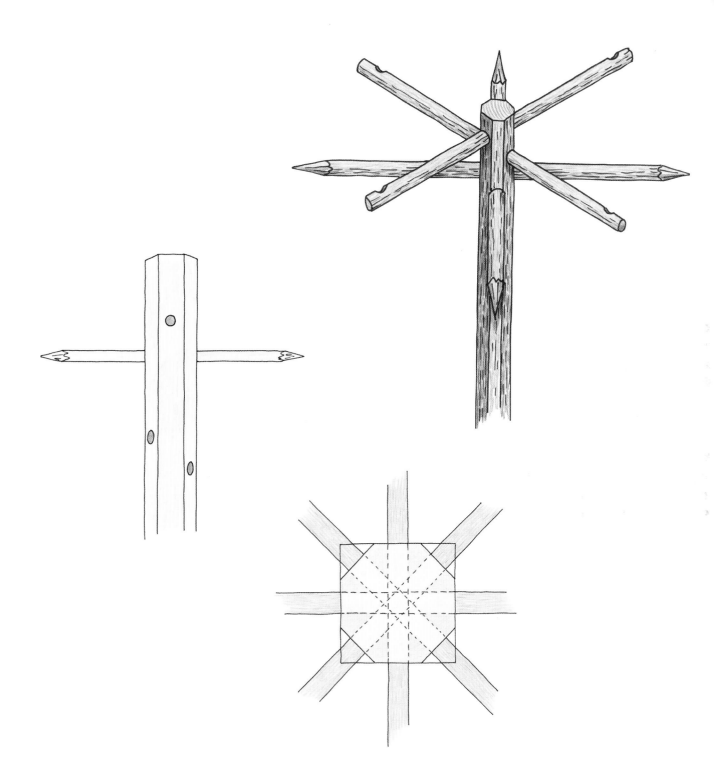

Nesting box

Nesting boxes are always a delightful addition to a garden. It is so exciting to see a pair of birds take up residence in a box and then to hear the little chirping sounds coming from inside. When the young birds are ready to fly they peek out of the box and thrilling days follow as they learn to master their skills. Different birds require different sized boxes and entry holes. We decided to have fun and create an amusing high-rise nesting box with room for several families. We attach our nesting boxes to trees by hanging them from flexible tie wire. Always avoid nailing or screwing your box to the tree, partly because you could damage the tree and partly because the nail or screw will grow into the tree and you won't be able to remove it properly when you decide to take down the nesting box.

MATERIALS

- blue tit box 22 x 145 mm (1 x 6 in): planed timber, 1.25 m (4 ft) long
- starling box 22 x 170 mm (1 x 7 in): planed timber, 1.65 m (5½ ft) long
- hole surround, 70 x 70 mm (3 x 3 in)
- tempered hardboard
- nails
- wood adhesive
- tie wire

INSTRUCTIONS

Cut the planks and nail or screw the pieces together to make a box (see illustration). You can make the high-rise box by nailing the floors to one of the sides and then nailing the other side in place. You could cover the roof with roofing felt or treat the wood to make it waterproof. If you like, you can cut a small square of harder material, such as waterproof board, to place around the entrance hole. That will protect the hole from water and wear and tear. Some nesting boxes have a short perch under the hole. You can make one of those from a length of thin dowel, drilling a small hole where you want it to be. You only need to fasten the back section at the top and the bottom of the box. Attach wire for hanging it up. Treat the exterior with oil, gloss or exterior paint.

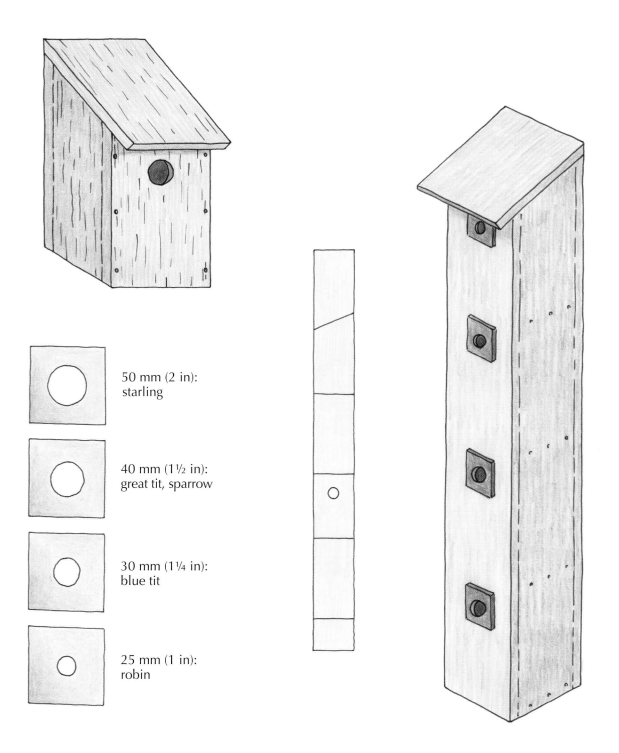

50 mm (2 in):
starling

40 mm (1½ in):
great tit, sparrow

30 mm (1¼ in):
blue tit

25 mm (1 in):
robin

Stair gate

With a stair gate parents with small children can avoid all the worry about little ones crawling to the stairs and falling down them. Here is a stair gate that is easy to install and will not leave large marks behind when the time comes to remove it. It is a good idea to have two gates: one at the bottom of the staircase and one at the top. A gate is also very useful to have in doorways, such as the door to a veranda or balcony, to stop children and even dogs from getting outside, while still being able to keep the door open. This stair gate consists of two uprights and a board. The uprights have a groove in the middle, and the board slides into them. The height is adapted to adults who can comfortably step over it without having to pull out the board every time they want to pass through.

MATERIALS
- 70 x 70 mm (3 x 3 in) planed timber, 1.4 m (5 ft)
- 22 x 22 mm (1 x 1 in) stripwood
- 12 mm (½ in) thick sheet plywood

INSTRUCTIONS
Cut the timber into two equal lengths. Screw these uprights to the wall on each side of the staircase or in a door opening. Attach two pieces of stripwood to each upright with glue and screws (see the illustration). Measure the distance between the uprights and make the width of the board to fit. Cut the board from plywood, with either a straight upper edge or a curved one, as illustrated. Finally, saw a hole in the board to make it easy to lift in and out.

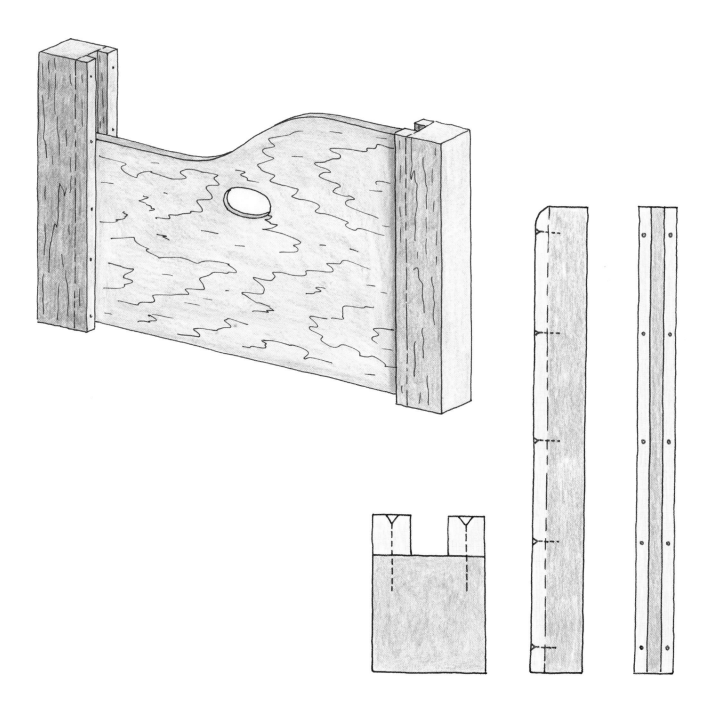

Balustrade

In some houses there are staircase balustrades and gallery levels which can cause problems for families with young children. Sometimes the space between the spindles is too wide, especially in older houses, and so it is not enough simply to block off the staircase top and bottom with a gate.

Close the gaps between the spindles by inserting dowel rods in the spaces. To ensure a child is not tempted to crawl between them and get stuck, there should be no more than 10 cm (4 in) between each spindle.

MATERIALS
- dowel of your chosen diameter
- skirting or stripwood if necessary
- wood adhesive or latex sealant
- paint for wood

INSTRUCTIONS

Saw the required number of dowel rods to suit the height of the banister. Drill one hole 40 mm (2 in) deep in the banister rail and another 20 mm (1 in) deep in the lower plinth. If there is no lower plinth and you don't want to drill a hole in the floor, cut lengths of timber and fit them between the existing spindles first. Then add skirting or stripwood to form a plinth along the length of the construction to give it a neat finish. Fill the holes with glue or latex sealant and insert the dowel. Begin with the deeper hole in the banister rail and then fit the dowel into the lower hole. Paint the dowel as required.

It is easy to remove the rods when the children are older. Knock each one gently to loosen the adhesive and then push it upwards and sideways. Hide any traces by blocking the holes with wood filler, sanding and then painting the balustrade – after all those years with small children it might well be time for a cosmetic renovation!

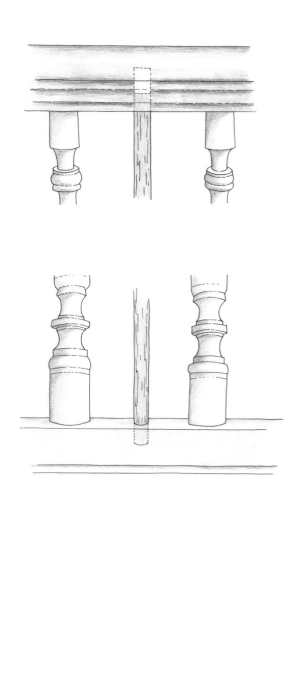

Further Reading

From Floris Books, Edinburgh unless
otherwise stated

Adolphi, Sybille, *Making Fairy Tale Scenes*
—, *Making Flower Children*
—, *Making More Flower Children*
Almon, Joan, *First Steps in Natural Dyeing*,
    WECAN Publications
Berger, Petra, *Feltcraft*
Berger, Thomas, *The Christmas Craft Book*
—, *Crafts Through the Year*
—, *The Gnome Craft Book*
Dhom, Christel, *The Advent Craft and Activity Book*
Fischer, Ute, *Weaving With Children*
Grigaff, Anne-Dorthe, *Knitted Animals*, Hawthorn
    Press
Guéret, Frédérique, *Magical Window Stars*
Jaffke, Freya, *Celebrating Festivals with Children*
—, *Toymaking with Children.*
—, *Work and Play in Early Childhood*
Jaffke, Freya & Dagmar Schmidt, *Magic Wool*

Kutsch, Irmgard & Brigitte Walden, *Winter
    Nature Activities for Children* (includes
    working with wood)
Leeuwen, M v. & J. Moeskops, *The Nature
    Corner: Celebrating the year's cycle with
    seasonal tableaux*
Neuschütz, Karin, *Creative Wool*
—, *Making Soft Toys*
—, *Sewing Dolls*
Reinhard, Rotraud, *A Felt Farm*
Schäfer, Christine, *Magic Wool Fairies*
—, *Magic Wool Fruit Children*
—, *Magic Wool Mermaids, Fairies and Nymphs
    Through the Seasons*
Wolck-Gerche, Angelika, *Creative Felt*
—, *More Magic Wool*
—, *Papercraft*

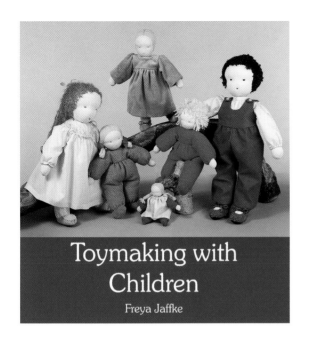

Toymaking with Children

Freya Jaffke

The Gnome Craft Book

Thomas and Petra Berger

Weaving With Children

Ute Fischer

The Nature Corner

Celebrating the year's cycle with seasonal tableaux

M. van Leeuwen and J. Moeskops

www.florisbooks.co.uk

Magic Wool
Creative Pictures and Tableaux with Natural Sheep's Wool

Freya Jaffke and Dagmar Schmidt

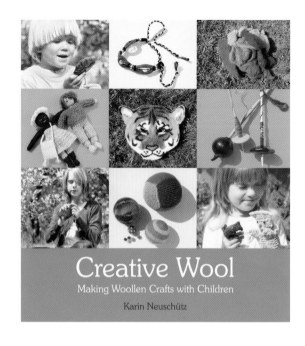

Creative Wool
Making Woollen Crafts with Children

Karin Neuschütz

Creative Felt
Felting and Making More Toys and Gifts

Angelika Wolk-Gerche

Feltcraft
Making Dolls, Gifts and Toys

Petra Berger

Magic Wool Fairies

Christine Schäfer

Magic Wool Fruit Children

Christine Schäfer

Magic Wool Mermaids, Fairies and Nymphs Through the Seasons

Christine Schäfer

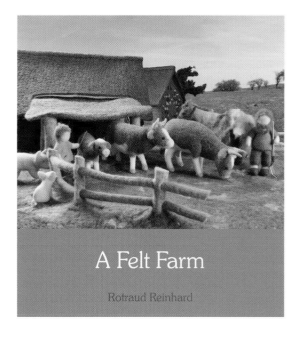

A Felt Farm

Rotraud Reinhard

www.florisbooks.co.uk

Making More Flower Children

Sybille Adolphi

Making Flower Children

Sybille Adolphi

The Christmas Craft Book

Thomas Berger

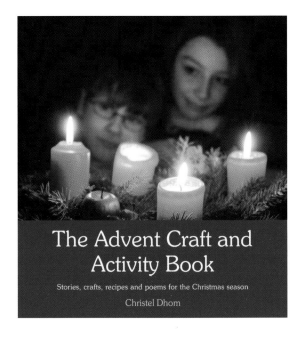

The Advent Craft and Activity Book

Stories, crafts, recipes and poems for the Christmas season

Christel Dhom